Kindle Fire™ HD

FOR

DUMMIES®

MINI EDITION

by Nancy C. Muir and Harvey Chute

WILEY

John Wiley & Sons, Inc.

Kindle Fire™ HD For Dummies® Mini Edition

Published by
John Wiley & Sons, Inc.
111 River Street
Hoboken, NJ 07030-5774
www.wiley.com

Copyright © 2013 by John Wiley & Sons, Inc., Hoboken, New Jersey

Published by John Wiley & Sons, Inc., Hoboken, New Jersey

Published simultaneously in Canada

For general information on our other products and services, please contact our Customer Care Department within the U.S. at 877-762-2974, outside the U.S. at 317-572-3993, or fax 317-572-4002.

For technical support, please visit www.wiley.com/techsupport.

Wiley publishes in a variety of print and electronic formats and by print-on-demand.

ISBN 978-1-118-53071-9 (paper)

10 9 8 7 6 5 4 3 2 1

WILEY

Contents at a Glance

iv

Publisher's Acknowledgments

We're proud of this book; please send us your comments at
http://dummies.custhelp.com. For other comments, please
contact our Customer Care Department within the U.S. at 877-762-
2974, outside the U.S. at 317-572-3993, or fax 317-572-4002.

Some of the people who helped bring this book to market include
the following:

Acquisitions and Editorial

Project and Copy Editor:
Jodi Jensen

Sr. Acquisitions Editor:
Katie Mohr

Technical Editor: Earl Boysen

Editorial Manager: Jodi Jensen

Cover image: © fleag/
iStockphoto.com (background)

Composition Services

Sr. Project Coordinator:
Kristie Rees

Layout and Graphics:
Christin Swinford

Proofreader:
Melissa D. Buddendeck

Publishing and Editorial for Technology Dummies

Richard Swadley, Vice President and Executive Group Publisher

Andy Cummings, Vice President and Publisher

Mary Bednarek, Executive Acquisitions Director

Mary C. Corder, Editorial Director

Publishing for Consumer Dummies

Kathleen Nebenhaus, Vice President and Executive Publisher

Composition Services

Debbie Stailey, Director of Composition Services

Introduction

● ●

Kindle Fire HD is a very affordable way to get at all kinds of media, from music and videos to books and colorful magazines. It's also a device that allows you to browse the Internet, check your e-mail, and read documents. Its portability makes it incredibly useful for people on the go in today's fast-paced world.

In this book, I introduce you to all the cool features of Kindle Fire HD, providing tips and advice for getting the most out of this ingenious little tablet. I help you find your way around its attractive and easy-to-use interface, and even recommend some neat apps that make your device more functional and fun.

Foolish Assumptions

Kindle Fire HD users come in all types. I won't assume in this book that you're a computer whiz, but I will assume that you have a passing understanding of how to copy a file and plug in a USB cable. I'm guessing you've browsed the Internet at least a few times and heard of Wi-Fi, which is what you can use to go online with a Kindle Fire HD. Other than that, you don't need a lot of technical background to get the most out of this book.

How This Book Is Organized

For Dummies books don't require a linear read, meaning that you could jump in anywhere and find out what you need to know about a particular feature. However, if you're opening the box and starting from square one with your Kindle Fire HD, consider working through the first part first. It provides information about setting up your Kindle Fire HD and navigating your way around its interface. Subsequent parts help you go online and then begin to explore the wealth of multimedia and written content Kindle Fire HD makes available to you.

Icons Used in This Book

Icons are little pictures in the margin of this book that alert you to special types of advice or information, including

 These short words of advice draw your attention to faster, easier, or alternative ways of getting things done with Kindle Fire HD.

 When you see this icon, you'll know that I'm emphasizing important information for you to keep in mind as you use a feature.

There aren't too many ways you can get into trouble with the Kindle Fire HD, but in those few situations, I include warnings so you avoid any pitfalls.

Get Going!

Time to get that Kindle Fire HD out of its box, set it up, and get going with all the fun, entertaining things it makes available to you. Have fun!

Part I

Getting "Fired" Up

•••••••••••••••••••••••••••••••••••

In This Part

▶ Comparing Kindle Fire HD to the competition

▶ Surveying and setting up Kindle Fire HD

▶ Playing with libraries, the Carousel, and Favorites

▶ Using a Micro USB cable

▶ Delving into all the settings Kindle Fire HD offers

•••••••••••••••••••••••••••••••••••

*A*mazon, the giant online retailer, just happens to have access to more content (music, movies, audio books, and so on) than just about anybody on the planet. Now, with its release of the second generation of its Kindle Fire tablet, and as Amazon continues to stack up media partnerships with the likes of Fox and PBS, the Kindle Fire is seen as the first real challenge to Apple's iPad.

The Kindle Fire HD is an awesome machine in its own right, one that provides the right price and feature mix for many people, while offering the key to that treasure chest of content Amazon has been wise enough to amass.

In this part, you get an overview of the Kindle Fire HD: how it compares to competing devices and its key features. You also get a quick introduction to the

Kindle Fire HD interface, touchscreen, and organization, as well as a first look at all the settings Kindle Fire HD offers.

How Kindle Fire HD Stacks Up to the Competition

A tablet is a handheld computer with an onscreen keyboard and apps that allow you to play games, read e-books, check e-mail, browse the web, and more. In the world of tablets, the first device to hit big was iPad; subsequent tablets, such as Samsung Galaxy, Google Nexus 7, and HP TouchPad, appeared a little later. The iPad has had the largest foothold in the market up to now, so the logical comparison here is to the iPad.

First, take a look at the Kindle Fire models currently available. You can choose from two display sizes: 7 inch and 8.9 inch. In addition, different configuration options are available for each Kindle Fire model, as shown in the following list:

- ✔ **Kindle Fire HD with 7-inch display.** Available with 16GB or 32GB memory.

- ✔ **Kindle Fire HD with 8.9-inch display.** Available with 16GB or 32GB memory.

- ✔ **Kindle Fire HD, 8.9-inch display with 4G LTE.** Available with 32GB or 64GB memory.

- ✔ **Kindle Fire (non-HD) with 7-inch display.** Available with 8GB memory.

With those options in mind, look at how Kindle Fire compares to iPad. All models of Kindle Fire HD are lighter and smaller than iPad. The 7-inch Kindle Fire HD (see Figure 1-1) weighs only 13.9 ounces, and the

8.9-inch Kindle Fire HD weighs only 20 ounces. This compares to iPad's 9.7-inch display and 1.44-pound frame. That smaller, lighter form factor makes the Kindle Fire HD easier to hold with one hand than the iPad.

Figure 1-1: The Kindle Fire HD is easy to hold.

The Kindle Fire HD 7-inch model has a projected battery life of eleven hours, versus iPad's ten hours. The high-definition screen resolution on the Kindle Fire HD's bright color screen is just about on par with the iPad screen; both tablets display pixels at a resolution that is finer than human eyes can detect.

Kindle Fire HD models have internal storage options from 16GB up to 64GB for the Kindle Fire HD 4G LTE. This is comparable to the 16, 32, or 64GB options for the various iPad models. Beyond that, Amazon provides free storage for all your Amazon-purchased content in the *Cloud* (a huge collection of online storage) so you can stream video and music instead of downloading it.

Kindle Fire HD also has some very intelligent technology that allows your browser to take advantage of the Cloud to display your web pages faster.

Kindle Fire HD has a front-facing camera, which currently is limited to use with Skype for video calls. It has a built-in microphone and dual stereo speakers. iPad has a microphone, a single speaker, and, unlike the Fire, both front-facing and back-facing cameras. iPad also has a built-in GPS, whereas Kindle Fire HD models use Wi-Fi for location services.

In several ways, Kindle Fire HD is easy to use, with a simple Android-based touchscreen interface. It's also a great device for consuming media — and what a lot of media Amazon makes available! Kindle Fire HD also offers Amazon's Silk browser, an e-mail client, and the fabulous Kindle e-reader (see Figure 1-2). So, despite the lack of a few preinstalled apps such as a calculator (which you can buy from the Amazon Appstore), with its dramatically lower price point, Kindle Fire HD may be the tablet of choice for many.

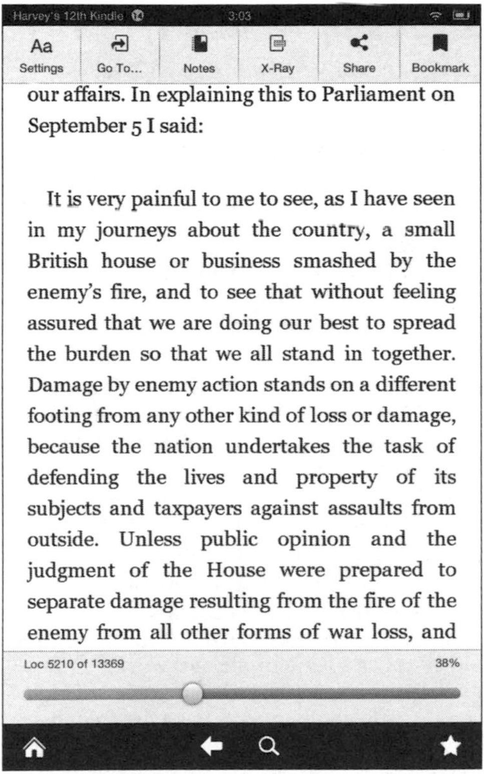
Harvey's 12th Kindle
3:03
Aa
Settings
Go To...
Notes
X-Ray
Share
Bookmark
our affairs. In explaining this to Parliament on September 5 I said:
It is very painful to me to see, as I have seen in my journeys about the country, a small British house or business smashed by the enemy's fire, and to see that without feeling assured that we are doing our best to spread the burden so that we all stand in together. Damage by enemy action stands on a different footing from any other kind of loss or damage, because the nation undertakes the task of defending the lives and property of its subjects and taxpayers against assaults from outside. Unless public opinion and the judgment of the House were prepared to separate damage resulting from the fire of the enemy from all other forms of war loss, and
Loc 5210 of 13369
38%

Figure 1-2: It all started with Kindle e-reader functionality.

Key Features of Kindle Fire HD

Kindle Fire HD is one spiffy little device with all the things most people want from a tablet packed into an easy-to-hold package: e-mail, web browsing, players for video and music content, an e-reader, a great online content store, access to tens of thousands of Android apps, and so on. Here is a brief look at all these great features:

- **Check out the price:** In case you didn't notice in the last section, Kindle Fire HD costs much less than the lowest-priced, newest iPad: $199 versus $499. 'Nuff said?

- **Preinstalled functionality:** The Kindle Fire HD comes out of the box with preinstalled apps such as an e-reader, music and video players, apps for Contacts, Calendar, OfficeSuite, and Skype, the Silk web browser, photo viewing, and an e-mail client. And those are just some of the apps!

- **The magic of Whispersync:** If you've ever owned a Kindle e-reader, you know that downloading content to it has always been seamless. All you need for this process is access to a wireless network. Then, you simply order a book, and within moments it appears on your Kindle device. Kindle Fire HD enjoys the same kind of easy download capability for books, music, video, and periodicals. Whispersync helps sync across various devices items such as bookmarks you've placed in an e-book or the last place you watched in a video.

✔ **Content, content, content!** Kindle Fire HD is intended as a device you use to consume media, meaning that you can play/read all kinds of music, movies, TV shows, podcasts, e-books, magazines, and newspapers. Amazon has built up a huge amount of content, from e-books (1.2 million titles and counting in the Kindle Store, shown in Figure 1-3), to movies and TV shows (120,000 movies and TV series), music (20 million songs), and hundreds of your favorite magazines.

✔ **The Amazon Silk browser:** Silk is Amazon's new browser; it's simple to use and has real performance benefits. Amazon Silk is touted as a "Cloud-accelerated split browser," which means that the browser can use the power of Amazon's servers to load the pages of a website quickly. You also get what's called a *persistent* connection. This means that your tablet is always connected to the Amazon Internet backbone (the routes data travels to move among networks online) whenever it has access to a wireless Internet connection.

✔ **Free Cloud storage:** Kindle Fire HD models have considerable storage space (up to 64GB). In addition to that, when you own a Kindle Fire HD, you get free, unlimited Cloud storage for all digital content purchased from Amazon (not content that you copy onto Kindle Fire HD from your computer by using a Micro USB cable). This means that books, movies, music, and apps are held online for you to stream or download at any time, instead of being stored on your device.

What is this

How do I store on Cloud or is it automatic when I purchase from Amazon

Figure 1-3: The Kindle Store offers more than 1 million books.

✔ **A world of color on the durable display:** The display on Kindle Fire HD offers a high-definition display and 16 million colors. The high-resolution screen makes for very crisp colors when you're watching that hit movie or reading a colorful magazine. In-plane switching (*IPS*) is a technology that gives you a wide viewing angle on the Kindle Fire HD screen. Amazon has taken IPS one step further by adhering a polarizing filter to the display, enabling vivid color and contrast to be displayed from any viewing angle. The result is that when you share your movie with a friend sitting next to you on the couch, she has no problem seeing what's on the screen from that side angle.

✔ **The value of Amazon Prime:** Kindle Fire HD comes with one free month of Amazon Prime. This service is a great deal. During your free month, Prime allows you to get perks such as free two-day shipping on thousands of items sold through Amazon, as well as free instant videos. If you decide to pick up the service after your free month, it costs you $79 a year. *Renew this each year*

Opening and Powering Your Kindle Fire HD

When your Kindle Fire HD arrives, it comes in an elegant black box. The Kindle Fire HD itself rests on top of a piece of hard plastic, and a small black card with some Kindle Fire HD basics printed on both sides is slotted into the lid of the box. Finally, beside the Kindle HD is a USB cable in a paper sleeve. That's it. Remove the protective plastic from the device, and you're ready to go.

After you get the tablet out of its packaging, it's time to turn it on. The Kindle Fire HD sports a Power button on the top of the device when you hold it in portrait orientation (see Figure 1-4). Next to the Power button are volume control buttons and a headphone jack.

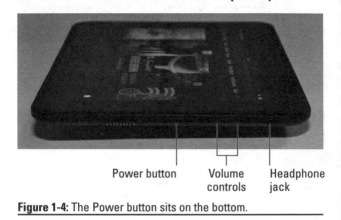

Power button   Volume controls   Headphone jack

Figure 1-4: The Power button sits on the bottom.

To turn the device on, press the Power button. If you're starting up for the first time, you're taken through a series of setup screens (see the following section for more about this). After you go through the setup process and register your Kindle Fire HD, you see the Home screen with a Status bar that gives you information about items such as your device's battery charge, the current time, wireless signal strength, and any notifications about recent downloads or apps installed.

If you want to lock your Kindle Fire HD, which is akin to putting a laptop computer to sleep, tap the Power button again. To shut down your Kindle, press and

hold the Power button until a message appears offering
you the option to Shut Down or Cancel.

 If your Kindle Fire HD becomes nonresponsive,
you can press and hold the Power button for
20 seconds, and it should come to life again.

Knowing the touchscreen

Before you work through the setup screens for your
Kindle Fire HD, it helps if you to get to know the basics
of navigating the touchscreen — especially if you've
never used a touchscreen before:

- Tap an item to select it or double-tap an item
  (such as an app) to open it.

- If your Kindle Fire HD goes to a lock screen after a
  period of inactivity, swipe your finger from right
  to left from the padlock icon (see Figure 1-5) to go
  to the Home screen.

- Double-tap to enlarge text and double-tap again to
  return the text to its original size. Note, this works
  only in certain locations, such as when you are
  displaying a web page in the Silk browser.

- Place your fingers apart on a screen and pinch
  them together to zoom in on the current view;
  place your fingers together on the screen and
  move them apart (unpinch) to enlarge the view.

- Swipe left to move to the next page in apps, such
  as the e-reader or the Silk web browser. Swipe to
  the right to move to the previous page.

- Swipe up and down to scroll up and down a web
  page or move from chapter to chapter in a book.

Unlock button

Figure 1-5: Swipe left from the Unlock button to go to the Home screen.

Setting up your Kindle Fire HD

When you turn Kindle Fire HD on for the first time, you see a series of screens that help you set up and register the device. Don't worry: There aren't many questions, and you know all the answers. The first screen is titled *Welcome to Kindle Fire.* This is the point in the setup process when you connect to a Wi-Fi network. You need this connection to register your device.

 At some point during this setup procedure you may be prompted to plug in your adapter if your battery charge is low. You also may be notified that the latest Kindle software is downloading, so you have to wait for that process to complete before you can move forward.

Follow these steps to register and set up your Kindle Fire HD:

1. **In the Connect to a Network list (shown on the screen in Figure 1-6), tap an available network.**

   Kindle Fire HD connects to the network (you may need to enter a password and then tap Connect to access an available network) and then displays the Register Your Kindle screen.

2. **On the Register Your Kindle screen that appears (see Figure 1-7), enter your Amazon account information (e-mail address and a password) and tap the Register button; then skip to Step 5.**

   Continue to Step 3 if you don't have an Amazon account.

3. **If you don't have an Amazon account, click the Create Account link.**

This link takes you to the Create an Amazon Account screen, with fields for entering your name, e-mail address, and password (which you have to retype to confirm).

4. **Enter this information, and then tap Continue.**

5. **If you want to read the terms of registration, tap the By Registering, You Agree to All of the Terms Found Here link.**

6. **When you finish reading the terms, tap the Close button to return to the registration screen.**

7. **To complete the registration, tap the Register button. At this point a "Select Your Time Zone" screen is displayed.**

Figure 1-6: Start by connecting to a Wi-Fi network.

Figure 1-7: Register your Kindle Fire HD to use it.

8. **Tap to select a time zone from the list provided.**

   For countries other than the United States, tap "Select another time zone" and choose from the provided list. Then tap the Back button in the bottom-left corner to return to the Time Zone screen.

9. **Tap Continue.**

   A final screen appears saying Confirm Account. You also see a link labeled Not <*Your Name*>? If, for some reason, you aren't you (for example, you may have entered your account information incorrectly), tap the Not <*Your Name*> link to change your account information. Otherwise, tap the Continue link.

The next screen displayed is the Get Started screen, which allows you to link your Kindle Fire HD with your Facebook and Twitter accounts. Doing so makes it easy to share recommendations with your friends and followers.

This is the point at which the Kindle Fire HD will likely download the latest Kindle software.

When the download finishes, you can view a series of quick tips to get you started with Kindle Fire HD.

Kindle Fire HD does much of what it does by accessing your Amazon account. You need to have an Amazon account to shop, access the Amazon Cloud library online, and register your Kindle Fire HD, for example. The My Account option in Settings provides information about the account to which the device is registered.

Charging the battery

Kindle Fire HD has a battery life of eleven hours for Wi-Fi–connected activities, such as web browsing, streaming movies, and listening to music from the Cloud. If you're a bookworm who's more into the printed word than media, you can get even more battery life with wireless turned off.

You charge the battery by using the provided charger. Attach the smaller end of the charger to your Kindle Fire HD's Micro USB port, located on the right side of the device, and the other end to a wall outlet. If Kindle Fire HD is completely out of juice, it takes about four hours to charge.

 You can check the battery indicator on the Status bar that runs across the top of the Kindle Fire HD screen to see if your battery is running low.

Getting to Know the Interface

The interface you see on the Kindle Home screen (see Figure 1-8) is made up of three areas. At the top, you see a set of buttons that takes you to the Kindle Fire HD libraries that contain various types of content. In the middle of the screen is the Carousel. The Carousel contains images of items you recently used that you can flick with your finger to scroll through and tap to open. Finally, the bottom portion of the Home screen shows items related to the center item in your Carousel. For example, it will show "Customers Also Bought" items related to the book, app, or music track in your Carousel.

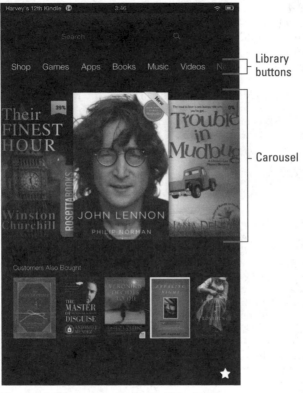

Figure 1-8: Move around with the flick of a finger.

Accessing Kindle Fire HD libraries

The Kindle Fire HD libraries are where you access downloaded content, as well as content stored by Amazon in the Cloud. Libraries (with the exception of the Docs library) also offer a Store button that you can tap to go online to browse and buy more content. Here are a few other things about content and libraries:

✔ **Tap any library button to open a library of downloaded and archived content:** Games, Apps, Books, Music, Videos, Newsstand, or Audiobooks. The Device tab shows you only content you have downloaded; the Cloud tab displays all your purchases or free content stored in Amazon's Cloud library, including content you've downloaded to the Kindle Fire HD.

✔ **The Video app opens to the Amazon store rather than a library:** In most cases, it's not very prudent to download video content to your Kindle Fire HD. Because this type of content takes up so much of your memory, it's preferable to play video from Amazon Cloud (which is called *streaming*).

✔ **You can download archived content at any time or remove downloaded content to the Cloud:** You can also view the contents of libraries in different ways, depending on which library you're in. For example, you can view Music library contents by categories such as Songs, Artists, Playlists, and Albums.

When you go to a library and tap the Cloud button, content currently downloaded sports a small check mark. You can download content by tapping the item at any time and then tapping Download.

Playing with the Carousel

If you've used an Android device, such as a smartphone, you've probably encountered the Carousel concept. On Kindle Fire HD, items you've used recently show up here chronologically, with the most recent item used on top (refer to Figure 1-8). You can swipe your finger to the right or left to flick through the Carousel contents. When you find an item you want to view or play, tap to open it.

Whatever you tap opens in the associated player or reader. Music opens in the Amazon MP3 music player; video in the Amazon Video player; and docs, books, and magazines in the Kindle e-reader.

 When you first begin using Kindle Fire HD, before you've accessed any content, the Carousel by default contains the Kindle User Guide. It may also contain recently used content from your Amazon Cloud library or content you've accessed from other registered Kindle devices that you may have.

Organizing Favorites

Sometimes the Kindle Fire HD's Carousel can get a bit crowded. You may have to swipe five or six times to find what you need. That's where Favorites comes in.

On the Kindle Fire HD, Favorites is a place for saving frequently used content. If, for example, you're reading a book you open often or you play a certain piece of music frequently, place it in the Favorites area of the Kindle Fire HD Home screen so you can find it more quickly. To pin an item to Favorites, press and hold it in the Carousel or a library, and then select Add to Favorites from the menu that appears. To remove content from Favorites, press and hold the item; then choose Remove from Favorites or Delete from the menu that appears.

To view favorites at any time, press the star-shaped button in the lower-right corner of the Home page.

Getting clues from the Status bar

The Status bar runs across the top of every Kindle Fire HD screen, just like the Status bar on your mobile phone. This bar, shown in Figure 1-9, provides the current time and information about your wireless connectivity and your battery charge. By swiping down on the Status bar, you can access your Kindle Fire HD settings.

| Harvey's 12th Kindle 🔞 | 3:59 | 🛜 🔋 |

Figure 1-9: Tools and settings on the Status bar.

Here's a rundown of what you'll find on the Status bar:

- ✔ **Device name:** First from the left end is the name of your Kindle Fire HD, such as Harvey's Kindle.

- ✔ **Notifications:** Sometimes, a number appears next to the name of your device. This number indicates how many Notifications you have pending — usually from the Kindle Fire HD system or an e-mail client. To view your notifications, swipe down on the Status bar.

- ✔ **Current time:** The next item on the Status bar is the current time, based on the time zone you specified when setting up the Kindle Fire HD.

- ✔ **Quick Settings:** Swipe down on the Status bar to access Quick Settings. Use these items to adjust

volume, brightness, or your Wi-Fi connection, for
example. To access the full Kindle Fire HD Settings
menu, tap More.

✔ **Wi-Fi Connection:** The item on the Status bar to
the right of Quick Settings is an icon showing you
the Wi-Fi connection status. If the icon is lit,
you're connected. The more bars in the symbol
that are bright white, the stronger the connection.

✔ **Battery charge:** Finally, the icon on the far right
indicates the charge remaining on your battery.

The ever-present, changing Options bar

The Options bar runs along the bottom of your Kindle
Fire HD screen. The items offered on the Options bar
change, depending on what library or app you're using,
but they always include a Home button. Additional items
such as Search let you run a search in features like a
content library. You almost always see a Menu button
when you tap the Options bar. This icon reveals commonly used actions, such as those for accessing settings
for the currently displayed feature. Figure 1-10 shows
you the options available on the Music library screen.

Using a Micro USB Cable to Transfer Data

It's easy to purchase or rent content from Amazon, but
you may want to get content from other places — such
as iTunes or the Pictures folder on your computer —
and play or view it on your Kindle Fire HD. To transfer
content to Kindle Fire HD, use the Micro USB cable that
came with your device. This cable has a USB connector
on one end and a Micro USB connector on the other.

Home button   Menu button   Search button

Figure 1-10: The Options bar with relevant options.

Attach the Micro USB end to your Kindle Fire HD (on the right side of the device) and the USB end to your computer.

 The right side of your Kindle Fire HD sports two port connectors: an HDMI-out port and a Micro USB port. They look similar and are unlabeled. The USB port is nearer the top of the device.

Your Kindle Fire HD should then appear as a drive in Windows Explorer or the Mac Finder. You can now click and drag files from your hard drive to the Kindle Fire HD or use the copy-and-paste functions to accomplish the same thing.

Using this process, you can transfer apps, photos, docs, music, e-books, and videos from your computer to your Kindle Fire HD. Then, just tap the relevant library (such as Books for e-books and Music for songs) to read or play the content on your Kindle Fire HD.

Opening Quick Settings

You access both a short list of commonly used settings and all the more detailed settings for Kindle Fire HD by swiping down in the Status bar area at the top of the screen. Here are the settings you can control from the Quick Settings menu (see Figure 1-11):

Figure 1-11: The settings that you access most often.

- ✔ **Unlocked/Lock:** This is a toggle feature, meaning that you tap it to lock your device into portrait or landscape mode.

- ✔ **Volume:** Tap Volume to display a slider bar that lets you increase or decrease the volume.

- ✔ **Brightness:** Use the slider beneath this setting to adjust the brightness manually. You can also tap the Automatic Brightness On/Off buttons to turn on or off a feature that controls the brightness of the screen based on ambient light.

- ✔ **Wireless:** Tap to display the Airplane Mode On/ Off button that you can use to turn wireless on or off. When you turn Wi-Fi on, a list of available networks appears. Tap an available network to join it. Note that you may be asked to enter a password to access some networks.

- ✔ **Sync:** If you've been out of range of a network, you might want to use this setting when you're back in range to manually initiate the download of new content or continue downloads that may have been interrupted.

Finding Other Settings

Beyond what I discuss in the preceding section, there is one more item on the Quick Settings menu — More. Many more settings appear when you tap the More button. These settings include: Help & Feedback, My Account, Applications, Parental Controls, Sounds & Display, Wireless, Device, Location-based Services, Keyboard, Security, and Legal & Compliance.

The way Kindle Fire HD works out of the box is usually very intuitive. But if you do find that you want to make an adjustment to settings, such as establishing parental controls, it's useful to know that all the settings shown in Figure 1-12 are available.

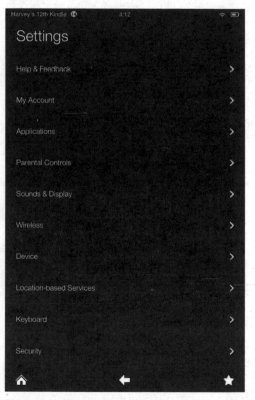

Figure 1-12: These settings appear when you tap More.

Part II

Online with the Kindle Fire HD

$\bullet \bullet$

In This Part

▶ Using your Amazon account

▶ Shopping at the Amazon Appstore

▶ Buying music, video, print, and anything

▶ Using Wi-Fi on your Kindle Fire HD

▶ Browsing the web with Silk

▶ Personalizing Silk's settings

$\bullet \bullet$

*K*indle Fire HD is, above all, a great device for consuming content, and buying that content or downloading free content is a key step to enjoying it. Amazon offers both a rich supply of books, magazines, music, and video, and an Amazon Appstore that lets you get your hands on apps that add to the functionality of your Kindle Fire HD. These apps can range from simple utilities such as a calculator to fun and addictive games and even a word processor or spreadsheet.

In addition, Amazon's Silk browser on your Kindle Fire HD can make it your new go-to device for staying informed and keeping in touch.

In this part, you can discover how to get apps, as well as books, magazines, music, and videos for your Kindle Fire HD. You also discover the ins and outs of browsing with Silk on Kindle Fire HD.

Managing Your Amazon Account

You buy things from Amazon by using the account and payment information you provide when you create an Amazon account. You probably have an account if you ever bought anything on Amazon (or opened an account when you bought your Kindle Fire HD). To buy things on Amazon with your Kindle Fire HD, your Amazon account must be associated with your Kindle Fire HD, and that happens during the setup process covered in Part I.

After you associate your device with an Amazon account, you can manage account settings by going to the Amazon website in the browser on either your Kindle Fire HD or computer and then tapping or clicking (depending on whether you're using a touchscreen device) Your Account at the top-right of the Amazon screen (see Figure 2-1). You can then tap/click Manage Payment Options or Add a Credit or Debit Card from the Payment section of your account and change or enter a new method of payment and billing address.

Figure 2-1: Managing your Amazon account on a PC.

Visiting the Amazon Appstore

After you create an Amazon account, you can shop for all kinds of content from your Kindle Fire HD. I'll start by introducing you to the world of apps. Apps provide you with functionality of all kinds, from an app that turns your Kindle Fire HD into a star-gazing instrument to apps that let you play a game. You can find calendar apps, drawing apps, and apps that provide maps so that you can find your way in the world.

Exploring the world of apps

The Amazon Appstore is full of apps written especially for devices based on the Android platform, including Kindle Fire HD. Follow these steps to explore the world of apps:

1. **Tap the Apps button at the top of the Home screen to enter your Apps library.**

2. **Tap the Store button and the store appears.**

   At the top of the store are links to various categories of apps. Below that is the offer *Today's Free App of the Day.*

3. **(Optional) Tap this option to download a free app to your device.**

The links at the top of the display are: Best Sellers, Games, New Releases, and All Categories.

 From the main Apps page you can see the Free App of the Day, Highly Rated Apps, and Recommended For You. The Recommended For You area shows personalized recommendations in that category based on your buying history.

Searching for apps

You can have fun browsing through categories of apps, but if you know which app you want to buy, using the search feature can take you right to it.

To search for an app, follow these steps:

1. **Tap in the Search Appstore field.**

   The keyboard shown in Figure 2-2 appears.

2. **Using the onscreen keyboard, enter the name of an app, such as the game Angry Birds Rio.**

   Suggestions appear beneath the Search field.

3. **Tap a suggestion to display the list of suggestions with more-detailed results, as shown in Figure 2-3.**

Figure 2-2: Search in the Appstore to find what you want.

4. **Tap an app name to see more details about it.**

You see screenshots from the app, along with a description, recommendations, customer reviews, product details, and developer info.

Figure 2-3: Search results in the Appstore.

Buying apps

You might find something you want by browsing or searching; when you're ready to buy, follow these steps:

1. **From the product description, tap the orange button that displays the price.**

   Note that if the app is free, this button reads Free, but if you have to pay for the app, the app price (such as $0.99) is displayed on the button. When you tap the button, the label changes to Get App.

2. **Tap the button again to purchase paid apps and download paid or free apps to your Kindle Fire HD.**

   A Downloading button appears, showing the download progress. When the installation is complete, an Open button appears.

3. **If you want to use the app immediately, tap the Open button.**

To use the app at any time, locate it in the App library; or, if you've used it recently, find it on the Carousel. Tap the app to open it; each app has its own controls and settings.

 You can buy apps from the Appstore on your PC or Mac. When placing the app in your shopping cart, be sure to select Kindle Fire HD as the device you want to download the app to in the drop-down list below the Add to Cart button.

To delete an installed app from your App library, press and hold it until a menu appears. Tap Remove from Device. The app isn't gone. It's still stored in the Cloud, and you can download it again at any time by tapping it in the Cloud tab of the App library.

Buying Content

Apps are great, but shopping for content is my favorite thing to do. I'm not putting down games and calculators, but to me, content means a night at the movies, a rainy afternoon with a good book, or a relaxing hour listening to a soothing collection of music. From Amazon, you can buy publications, books, music, and video (movies and TV shows) to download or stream to your Kindle Fire HD. The buying process is somewhat similar for the different types of content, but there are slight variations, which I go into in the following sections.

Buying publications through Newsstand

If you tap Newsstand on the Home page of Kindle Fire HD, and then tap the Store button, you see several categories of items. First, Featured Magazines are displayed across the top. Below Featured Magazines, you see magazine covers for free issues and best sellers. In the column on the right, you see browse options for Magazines and Newspapers, followed by categories. Categories include Arts & Photography, Automotive, Computers & Gaming, Cooking, Food & Wine, Family & Parenting, and many more. Tap the All Magazines button to see a complete list of available magazines.

When you find the publication you want, follow these steps to buy or subscribe to it:

1. **Tap the item.**

   A screen appears showing pricing, a description of the publication, and Subscribe Now and Buy Issue buttons (see Figure 2-4).

2. **Tap Subscribe Now or Buy Current Issue.**

The button changes to a box showing the Downloading status. When the download is complete, the button label changes to Read Now.

3. **Tap the Read Now button to open the magazine.**

Note that the magazine is stored in your Amazon Cloud library, where you can read or download it to your Kindle Fire HD at a later time.

Buying books

To browse through e-books from Amazon on your Kindle Fire HD, follow these steps:

1. **Tap the Books button on the Kindle Fire HD Home screen.**

2. **Tap the Store button.**

The Amazon Bookstore sports a Recommended for You section at the top, recommending books based on your buying history.

3. **Swipe right to left to scroll horizontally through the recommendations at the top.**

As with the Newsstand, when you locate and tap an item in the bookstore, you see a screen with that item's pricing and description. In the bookstore, the buttons you see at this point are labeled Buy for (price), Try a Sample, and Add to Wish List. Here's how these three buttons work:

✔ **Buy for (price):** Tap this button and it changes to a Downloading meter and then to a Read Now button. Tap the Read Now button to open the book. Remember that the book is now stored in your Books library where you can tap it to open and read it at your leisure.

Figure 2-4: Publication details and related buttons.

- ✔ **Try A Sample:** Tap this button and it changes to a Processing message and then to a Read Now button. Tap the Read Now button to open the sample of the book.

- ✔ **Add to Wish List:** Tap this button and a small form appears where you can select a Wish List; then press OK. The book is added to your Amazon Wish List where you can find it later to sample or buy.

Buying music

Tap the Music button on the Kindle Fire HD Home screen and then tap the Store button. On the Store screen, various features are displayed, such as New Releases, any special promotions, and Recommended For You. On the right side of the screen you see the following links: Bestsellers, New Releases, and Genres. Tap one of these links to get a list of items in that category. You can also tap the Albums or Songs tabs to view music by these criteria.

From anywhere in the Music Store, you see thumbnails of music selections. Follow these steps to buy music:

1. **Tap an item.**

   A screen appears, displaying a list of the songs in the case of an album with Price buttons for both the entire album and each individual song.

2. **Tap the arrow button to the left of a song to play a preview of it.**

3. **Tap a Price button.**

   The button label changes from the price of the item to the word Buy.

4. **Tap the Buy button.**

   The song or album downloads to your Music library. A confirmation dialog box opens, displaying a Go to Your Library button and a Continue Shopping button.

5. **Tap the Go to Your Library button to open the album and display the list of songs.**

   The album is now stored in both your Music library and the Cloud; if you tap on a song to play it, it'll also appear with recently accessed content in the Carousel.

 If you tap the Continue Shopping button, you can later find the album in your Music library.

Buying video

When you tap Video on the Kindle Fire HD Home screen, you're instantly taken to the Amazon Video Store shown in Figure 2-5.

Along with any special promotions, you see thumbnails of items in various categories, including Prime Instant Video, Next Up, Movies, TV Shows, and For the Kids. Each of these categories has a horizontally scrolling list of thumbnails for videos.

Tap an item, and a descriptive screen appears. For TV shows, this screen includes episode prices and a set of Season tabs. For movies, this screen offers a Watch Trailer button and purchase/rental options such as Rent, Rent HD, Buy, and Buy HD. The available purchase/rental options vary for different movies.

Figure 2-5: Shop for video in the Amazon Video Store.

Shopping for Anything Else

Amazon kindly preinstalled an Amazon Shopping app on your Kindle Fire HD. Tap the Shop link on the Home page. A screen opens with a dynamically changing featured item. Below that are shopping links for Digital items as well as physical products.

Proceed to shop as you usually do on Amazon, tapping any item of interest to add it to your cart and using your Amazon account information to pay and arrange for shipping.

Getting Online by Using Wi-Fi

All Kindle Fire HD models have Wi-Fi features, meaning that if you have access to a nearby Wi-Fi network, you can use that to go online. You might access a Wi-Fi connection through your home network, at work, or via a public hotspot, such as an Internet cafe or airport.

 In addition, the Kindle Fire HD 4G LTE has wireless access through the cellular data network. This requires a prepaid service plan for cellular data access.

When you first set up your Kindle Fire HD (as described in Part I), you can choose a Wi-Fi network to use for getting online. If you want to log on to a different network, follow these steps:

1. **Swipe down from the top of the screen to open a menu of common settings, such as Volume, Brightness, and Wireless.**

2. **Tap Wireless and the wireless settings appear.**

3. **Tap a network in the list of available wireless networks to sign in.**

   You have to enter a password to sign in to some networks.

Browsing with Silk

Silk is a browser that takes advantage of Amazon's capability to use its own servers to make your browsing experience fast.

The Silk browser recognizes browsing patterns and holds the next page in its cache (a dedicated block of memory) to deliver it quickly to you if you also make this selection. This capability makes your browsing experience fast and smooth as, well, silk.

Using navigation tools to get around

From the Kindle Fire HD Home screen, swipe left to scroll to the right in the list of links at the top until you see the Web link. Tap on the Web link to see Silk, as shown in Figure 2-6.

You can tap the Back Arrow and Forward Arrow icons to move among pages you've previously viewed. To go to Full-Screen Mode, press the button that looks like four outward-pointing arrows. (Click the equal sign button that pops up at the bottom of the screen to return to regular screen mode.)

To go directly to a page, tap in the Address field (note that this field acts as a Search field if you enter a word or phrase, or as an Address field if you enter a website's address — URL). Enter a site address and tap Go. The website is displayed.

Silk uses tabs that allow you to display more than one web page at a time and move among those pages. Tap the Add Tab button — which features a plus sign (+) — to add a tab in the browser. When you do, thumbnails of recently visited sites appear. You can tap on a thumbnail to go to that site, or you can tap in the Address bar and enter a URL by using the onscreen keyboard that appears.

Bookmarking sites

You can bookmark sites in Silk so that you can easily jump back to those sites again. With a site displayed onscreen, tap the Add Bookmark button to the left of the Address bar. In the Add Bookmark dialog box, tap OK to bookmark the displayed page.

Searching for content on a page

Web pages can contain a lot of content, so it's not always easy to find the article or discussion you want to view on a particular topic. To search the currently displayed page by using Silk, follow these steps:

1. **Tap Menu on the Options bar.**

2. **On the screen that appears, tap Find in Page.**

   The onscreen keyboard appears with the Search field active.

3. **Type a search term.**

   It appears in an orange box hovering above the first instance of the word on the page. Other instances of the word on that page are highlighted in yellow.

4. **Tap the Up or Down arrow beside the search field to jump to the next instance of the word.**

5. **Tap Done to end the search.**

Address/
Search field

Back   Forward   Full-Screen   Menu
Mode

Figure 2-6: Silk offers a familiar browser interface.

Searching the web

Most of us spend a lot of our time online browsing around to find what we want. Search engines make our lives easier because they help us narrow down what we're looking for by using specific search terms; they then troll the web to find matches for those terms from a variety of sources. To search the entire web, follow these steps:

1. **Tap the plus sign (+) to add a tab in the browser if you want search results to appear on a new tab.**

   Thumbnails of recently visited sites appear.

2. **Tap in the Search field.**

   The thumbnails change to a list of bookmarked sites or recently visited sites, and the onscreen keyboard appears.

3. **Enter a Search term and tap Go.**

   By default, search results appear in Bing.

4. **Tap a result to go to that page.**

Personalizing Silk

Silk sports a nice, clean interface. Still, there are a few things you can do to personalize the way Silk looks and acts that might work better for you. With Silk open, tap the Menu button on the Options bar, and then tap Settings. In the screen that appears, you see a couple of things you can control in the Silk interface:

- ✔ **Requested Website View:** Lets you specify mobile or desktop versions of websites or have the browser decide automatically.

- ✔ **Load Images:** Allows images on web pages to be displayed in the browser.

Part III

Kindle Fire HD in Action

• •

In This Part

▶ Looking into what's available to read

▶ Opening a good book or periodical

▶ Watching video on Kindle Fire HD

▶ Playing music

• •

K indle Fire HD comes from a family of e-readers, so it's only natural that the e-reader you use to read books and magazines on the device is a very robust feature. The device's bright, crisp screen also makes it a great device for playing video, both movies and TV shows. You can easily hold the Kindle Fire HD in one hand, and it's capable of streaming video from the Amazon Cloud, making a typically seamless viewing experience without hogging memory on the tablet itself.

In addition, Kindle Fire HD's capacity to tap into Amazon's tremendous Music Store and let you sideload music from other sources lets you build up your ideal Music library and take it with you wherever you go.

In this part, you discover what reading material is available, how you open publications, and how to read and then delete them from Kindle Fire HD when you're done. You also learn about getting video and music content onto your Kindle Fire HD and enjoying that content once it's there.

So Many Things to Read!

Kindle Fire HD makes it easy for you to buy your content from Amazon (as described in Part II). Although you can buy and sideload content from other sources to Kindle Fire HD, buying from Amazon ensures that you're dealing with a reputable company and receiving safe content (uncontaminated by malware).

You can also buy content at the Amazon website from your computer and have it download to your Kindle Fire HD. Just select what device you want it delivered to from the drop-down list below the Add to Cart button before you buy Kindle content.

Reading Books

After you own some Kindle books, you can begin to read by using the simple e-reader tools in the Kindle e-reader app. You may have used this app on another device, such as your computer, smartphone, or tablet, though each version of this app has slightly different features. In the following sections, you see how the Kindle Fire HD e-reader app works.

You can get to the Home screen from anywhere in the e-reader app. If a Home button isn't visible, just tap the bottom of the page to display the Options bar, which includes a Home button.

Going to the (Books) library

When you tap Books on your Kindle Fire HD Home screen, you open the Books library, containing downloaded content on the Device tab and content in the Cloud on the Cloud tab (see Figure 3-1). The active tab is the one displaying orange text. You can also use the Store link to go to Amazon's website and shop for books.

Several features in your Books library offer different perspectives on its contents:

- ✔ **Grid and List views.** Tap Menu on the Options bar to display the Grid View and List View options, which show your books by using large thumbnails on a bookshelf or in a text list including title and author, and a small thumbnail.

- ✔ **Sort titles.** Use the By Author, By Recent, and By Title buttons to view books by that criteria.

- ✔ **Identify new titles.** If you've just downloaded but haven't started reading a book, you see a gray banner in the corner of the thumbnail with the word New in it.

Opening a book

To open a book from the Home screen, tap Books to open the Books library. Locate the book you want to read (swipe upward if you need to reveal more books in the list) and simply tap it. If the book has not been downloaded to your Kindle Fire HD, it begins to download and takes only seconds to complete.

Cloud tab   Device tab   Store

Figure 3-1: All your book purchases on two tabs.

If you've never begun to read the book, it opens on its title page. If you've read part of the book, it opens automatically to the last page you read.

 You can also open a publication from Favorites or the Carousel. Read more about these features in Part I.

Navigating a book

An open book just begs to be read. You're used to flipping pages in a physical book, but an e-reader provides you with several ways to move around it. The simplest way to move one page forward or one page back is to tap your finger anywhere on the right or left side of the page, respectively. With a book page displayed, tap it near the center of the page to see the tools shown in Figure 3-2, including a button to take you to the Kindle Fire HD Home screen, a Back button to go back to the previous screen, a Search button to initiate a search for text in the book, and the Favorites "star" icon to bring up your favorite items.

You can also tap the Go To button in the Options bar and choose from these options to move around your book:

- ✔ **Go to Page or Location:** A pop-up appears, asking for a page or location. Enter the desired page or location, and press the appropriate button (Page or Location).

- ✔ **Sync to Furthest Page:** Moves you to the most recent page you read in the book with any Kindle reader app or device.

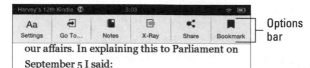

Options bar

our affairs. In explaining this to Parliament on September 5 I said:

It is very painful to me to see, as I have seen in my journeys about the country, a small British house or business smashed by the enemy's fire, and to see that without feeling assured that we are doing our best to spread the burden so that we all stand in together. Damage by enemy action stands on a different footing from any other kind of loss or damage, because the nation undertakes the task of defending the lives and property of its subjects and taxpayers against assaults from outside. Unless public opinion and the judgment of the House were prepared to separate damage resulting from the fire of the enemy from all other forms of war loss, and

Loc 5210 of 13369   38%

Progress bar

Home   Back   Search   Favorites

Figure 3-2: The page of a book in Kindle e-reader.

- ✔ **Beginning:** Return to the beginning of the book.

- ✔ **Cover:** Jump to the book's cover.

- ✔ **Table of Contents:** Each item in the table of contents is listed (as long as the publisher has provided a table of contents). Just tap a section to jump to it.

- ✔ **End:** Tap the End link to go to the end of the book where the Before You Go page is displayed. This page allows you to review and rate the book and share your thoughts through social media.

 The progress bar along the bottom of the screen indicates how far along in the publication you are at the moment. To move around the publication, you can press the circle on this bar and drag it in either direction.

Searching in a book

Want to find that earlier reference to a character so that you can keep up with a plot? Or do you want to find any mention of Einstein in an e-encyclopedia? Use the Search feature, as follows:

1. **With a book open, tap the center area of the page to display the Options bar, if necessary.**

2. **Tap the Search button in the Options bar at the bottom of the screen.**

   The Search dialog box and onscreen keyboard are displayed.

3. **Enter a search term or phrase, and then tap the Go key on the keyboard.**

   Search results are displayed, and the search term is indicated with a highlight.

Bookmarking your place in a book

If you find that perfect quote or a section you just have to read again at a later time, you can bookmark it by using the Bookmark feature.

To place a bookmark on a page, display the page and tap it to reveal the Bookmark button in the top-right corner of the page; then tap the Bookmark button. A small bookmark ribbon appears on the page.

Highlighting text

To highlight text, press and hold your finger at the beginning of the text, and drag your finger to the end of the text. The selected text is highlighted in blue.

Small gray handles appear on either side of the selected text. If you want to select additional adjacent text to be highlighted, press your finger on one of these handles and drag to the left or right.

A set of buttons appears above the selected text. Press Note to add a note, press Highlight to highlight the text, or press Share to post the selected text to social media.

Press More to bring up a set of options to Search for the selected text in the book, on Wikipedia, or on the web.

You can display a list of bookmarks and highlights by tapping the Notes button in the Option bar.

Modifying the appearance of a page

There are several things you can do to control how things appear on a page in Kindle e-reader. First, you can make text larger or smaller. You can choose a white, black, or sepia-toned background for a page. And finally, you can change the font type.

To control all these settings, tap the page to display the Options bar; then tap the Settings button (the one with a capital and lowercase A). The following options appear:

- ✔ **Font Size:** Tap the large or the small font button to progressively increase or decrease the font size.

- ✔ **Color Mode (black on white, black on sepia, white on black):** Tap a setting to display a different color page background. A sepia background, for example, may make reading easier on your eyes.

- ✔ **Font:** Change the font to one of five different font types.

- ✔ **Text-to-Speech:** Turn on or off the automatic reading of the book by the Text-to-Speech function.

Managing publications

After you purchase content on Amazon, from apps to music and books, it's archived in your Amazon Cloud library. If you finish reading a book on Kindle Fire HD, you can remove it from your device. The book is still in the Amazon Cloud, and you can re-download it to your Kindle Fire HD at any time.

To remove a book or magazine from your Book library, follow these steps:

1. **Tap Books or Newsstand to display your library.**

2. **Locate and press your finger on the item.**

   A menu appears (see Figure 3-3). Book samples offer only a Delete option in this menu. The pre-installed *New Oxford American Dictionary* offers only the option of adding it to Favorites.

Figure 3-3: Removing a publication from Kindle Fire HD.

The thumbnail of the removed item remains in your Books library on the Cloud tab and on the Carousel or Favorites if you've placed it there. To download and read the book again, just double-tap it in any of these locations, and the download begins.

Reading Periodicals

Reading magazines and newspapers on your Kindle Fire HD is similar to reading books, with a few important differences. You navigate magazines a bit differently and can display them in two different views. Follow these steps to read a magazine or newspaper:

1. **From the Home screen, tap Newsstand.**

2. **Tap a magazine or newspaper in the Newsstand (or Carousel) to read it.**

   If the publication hasn't been downloaded to the device, it begins to download now.

   With the Options bar visible, thumbnails of all pages in the publication are displayed along the bottom of the screen (see Figure 3-4).

3. **Swipe right or left to scroll through these pages.**

4. **When you find the page you want, tap that page to display it full screen.**

   The Menu button on the Options bar displays contents of the current issue.

5. **Tap the Table of Contents icon in the lower part of the screen, and tap an item in the table of contents to go to that item.**

Some periodicals can appear in two views:

- ✔ **Text view:** In Text view, you see articles in more of an e-reader format (meaning that you get larger text with no columns and no images).

- ✔ **Page view:** Page view shows an exact image of the publication's pages, with all columns and photos intact.

Tap the Page View or Text View button in the top-right corner of a displayed periodical to switch between these views (if the periodical offers this feature).

Figure 3-4: Scroll through thumbnails of pages.

Opening and Playing a Video

Playing a video is a simple process. If the video has been downloaded to your Kindle Fire HD, open the library (tap Video, and then tap the Library button), locate the video, and then tap the video to play it.

If you're streaming a video you've purchased from the Cloud, follow these steps:

1. **Tap the Cloud tab.**

   Videos you've rented (whose rental period hasn't expired) or purchased are displayed.

2. **Tap an item to open it.**

   If it's a TV show, you see episodes listed; tap one to open it. If it's a movie, at this point, you see a description of the movie.

3. **Tap the Watch Now button.**

   The playback controls appear.

4. **If you've already watched part of the video, tap the Resume button.**

The familiar playback tools available here include Play, Pause, a progress bar, a volume slider, and a button that moves you ten seconds back in the video.

Playing Music

After you have some music available, locate the item to play; then, use the playback toolbar to control the playback. Follow these steps to play music from your Music library:

1. **Tap the Music button on the Kindle Fire HD Home screen.**

2. **Locate an item you want to play on a tab in the Music library, such as Songs or Artists.**

3. **If you open a tab other than Songs, you need to tap to open an album or playlist to view the contents.**

4. **Tap to play the item.**

   If you tap the first song in a group of music selections, such as an album or playlist, Kindle Fire HD begins to play all selections, starting with the one you tapped.

5. **Use the controls shown in Figure 3-5 to control playback.**

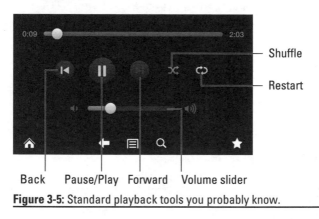

Figure 3-5: Standard playback tools you probably know.